San Francisco Museum of Modern Art

Photographs by Richard Barnes

Text by Justin Henderson

When the San Francisco Museum of Modern Art's new building
opened in 1995, it marked a fundamentally transformative event—clearly for the institution (which was celebrating its sixtieth anniversary), but more than that, for the city of San Francisco and for the international art community.

For SFMOMA, the building provided a doubling of gallery space, facilities for expanded educational and public programming, and state-of-the-art quarters for the full range of activities visitors expect in a museum today. Beyond this, the new Mario Botta–designed building meant that the Museum at last had a magnificent physical identity that announced to the world that this is a place of bold expression, of serious exploration, of dynamic public interaction and exchange. Indeed, the building has become a signal work in the Museum's collection—one that embodies all the attributes of great modern art.

The new SFMOMA became an immediately recognized icon in the cityscape, and one of the most visited attractions for tourists and residents alike. The new Museum also anchors the rapidly changing south of Market district. In just ten years, the area has changed from one which concerned many Museum trustees as a location for the building—since many San Franciscans rarely crossed Market Street to enter what was then Skid Row—to one of its most vibrant and active neighborhoods. Perhaps most revealing, SFMOMA has assumed a place of central importance in the life of the city, achieving the status of one of the few modern art museums in the world to attract a level of attendance and attention equal to its sister institutions with general interest or encyclopedic collections.

The place of the San Francisco Museum of Modern Art in the international art community is no less primary. SFMOMA is now a venue of choice for exhibitions traveling from around the world, and its programs in a wide range of areas—from its groundbreaking developments in interactive educational technologies to its distinguished conservation studio—are leading the field. Happily, in the last few years, the effort to construct this glorious building has inspired a wave of generosity for acquisitions to the permanent collection, and the Museum's holdings are now approaching a level of distinction that matches its extraordinary architecture.

As the still relatively new director of the San Francisco Museum of Modern Art—beginning my tenure three years after the opening of the new building—I can view these accomplishments with awe as well as pride. With this spectacular building, SFMOMA has proven that great monuments can still be built and San Francisco has demonstrated that cities still know how to do great things.

David A. Ross
Director

Looking through the turret wall toward the center stairs and fourth-floor galleries, with work by Mariko Mori in foreground

Mario Botta

I think a relationship based on dialogue is imperative between the architecture and the works of art. The works of art require optimal spaces to be completely enjoyed and, likewise, the gallery spaces need the works of art in order to acquire their full dimensions. In museums, the real challenge is to discover that perfect balance where the architecture and art enrich one another.

The atrium, the true heart of the building, is the center of spatial gravity for the entire Museum. Within its interior, the organization and spatial relationships of all those parts that surround and define should be perceived. It is the point from which visitors have access to the Museum's various functions and levels. It is an architectonically drawn space, with the light from above serving as a type of cornice for the protagonist—the Museum visitor. The galleries, on the upper levels, offer a subdued and calm architecture, which, as a result of the skylights, devote their space to the other protagonist—the work of art.

In today's city, the museum plays a role analogous to that of the cathedral of yesterday. A place of common encounter and confrontation. A place we require in order to challenge the hopes and contradictions of our time.

It is also a place where the values and aesthetics of the past are very much present and where the unique sensibilities of mankind are born witness throughout history. In fact, it might be possible to interpret the museum as a space dedicated to witnessing and searching for a new religiosity, which promotes and enriches those spiritual values that we so strongly need.

Mario Botta
Architect

The War Memorial Veterans Building shortly after the Museum opened in 1935

In 1995 the San Francisco Museum of Modern Art (SFMOMA) celebrated sixty rich, colorful years of West Coast art history with the opening of its splendid new building in San Francisco's south of Market district. It is now clear that this building has served to raise an already dynamic, well-regarded institution to a higher level of excellence. Over the course of sixty-five years, in its original location and in the new building, SFMOMA has established itself as one of the most forward-looking cultural institutions in the country, offering art lovers the challenge of groundbreaking new work as well as the enticements of an expanding collection of modern masterpieces.

With the decision to create a new home for its collection, the San Francisco Museum of Modern Art made another major cultural contribution to the nation. The second-largest structure in the United States devoted to modern and contemporary art, the modernist building designed by Swiss architect Mario Botta is a significant architectural landmark in San Francisco.

This contemporary structure of steel, glass, brick, and polished stone, anchoring one of the city's liveliest neighborhoods, has its roots in a venerable late-nineteenth-century institution. The San Francisco Art Association was founded in 1871 and three years later created the California School of Design—the first art school in the western United States—later to become the San Francisco Art Institute, which still thrives today. In 1918 the Art Association joined with the Musical Association of San Francisco to construct a performing-arts hall and an art-museum complex in the Civic Center. The Opera House and War Memorial Veterans Building were completed in the fall

of 1932, and in October 1934 the Museum's first curator, Grace L. McCann Morley, was appointed. (She was named director a few months later.)

The San Francisco Museum of Modern Art's new home opened to the public in 1995.

On opening day, January 18, 1935, the San Francisco Museum of Art, as it was first called, became the third American museum (after New York's Museum of Modern Art and the Phillips Collection in Washington, D.C.) committed to celebrating the new in international modern art. Propelling San Francisco into the dynamic, contentious world of contemporary art and setting a progressive standard for the visual arts in the western United States, the Museum introduced its Bay Area audience to provocative ideas and developments from major art centers on the East Coast and in Europe and also supported local artists by exhibiting their work.

The Museum's inaugural presentation offered a rich diversity of subjects, ranging from the Art Association's annual exhibition of work by its members to French Impressionist and Post-Impressionist painting, Chinese art, old master drawings, and Gothic tapestries. However, it was the Museum's second exhibition—the *1934 Carnegie International,* featuring contemporary European and American works—that established its progressive mandate. This was followed by groundbreaking exhibitions such as *Cubism and Abstract Art* (1936) and *Fantastic Art, Dada, and Surrealism* (1937), both organized by New York's Museum of Modern Art, and a survey of the work of Paul Cézanne (1937), organized by Morley. By 1940 the institution could boast 130,000 visitors annually.

The Museum continued to explore new artistic terrain in the 1940s and

1950s, presenting important solo exhibitions of the work of Arshile Gorky (1941), Clyfford Still (1943), Jackson Pollock (1945), Mark Rothko (1946), and Robert Motherwell (1946), heralding the emergence of Abstract Expressionism in American art. *Picasso: Forty Years of His Art* complemented the Museum's presentation in 1939 of the artist's masterpiece *Guernica;* exhibitions of the work of Bay Area artists David Park, Elmer Bischoff, and Hassel Smith celebrated artistic developments on the Museum's home ground.

Morley's tenure saw a significant expansion of the Museum's collections. Major acquisitions included paintings by Arshile Gorky, Vasily Kandinsky, Mark Rothko, Clyfford Still, Max Ernst, Paul Klee, and Jackson Pollock. In 1950 the Museum celebrated its fifteenth birthday with the bequest of the Harriet Lane Levy Collection, including works by Henri Matisse and Pablo Picasso. Under Morley, the institution became one of the first to recognize photography as a fine-art form. Augmenting this new direction for the growing collection was Trustee Albert M. Bender's 1941 bequest of twenty-six images by Ansel Adams, Brett and Edward Weston, and Imogen Cunningham, among others; in 1952 sixty-eight photographs by Alfred Stieglitz were acquired.

Morley relinquished her duties in 1958, but her legacy of progressive leadership defined the Museum's style in the following decades. The institution's subsequent directors, as well as its many curators, have all contributed to the growth of the permanent collection and the wide range of exhibitions, while maintaining the Museum's long-standing commitment to new developments in art.

The arrival of Henry T. Hopkins as director in 1974 set a dynamic new tone. Challenged by the lively art scene in Los Angeles, Hopkins sought to establish the Museum as the West Coast's premier showcase for twentieth-century art. His efforts to have the institution renamed led to its becoming the San Francisco Museum of Modern Art in 1975, reflecting the identity established during its earliest years. Hopkins committed the institution to embracing performance art, Conceptual art, and media arts, securing for SFMOMA a place on the cutting edge of new developments.

The year 1980 saw the organization of the landmark show *Avant-Garde Photography in Germany: 1919–1939* and the establishment of a Department of Photography, affirming SFMOMA's commitment to the medium. Photography shows soon accounted for one-third of SFMOMA's exhibition schedule.

Noteworthy painting exhibitions were also highlights of the 1980s, beginning with a retrospective of the work of Philip Guston. The Museum's ongoing dedication to exploring the roots of Modernism was reflected in such exhibitions as *Expressionism: A German Intuition, 1905–1920* (1981), co-organized with the Guggenheim Museum in New York; *Edward Hopper: The Art and the Artist* (1981); *Kandinsky in Munich: 1896–1914* (1982); and *Diego Rivera: The Cubist Years* (1984).

The Department of Architecture and Design was established in 1983, making its debut with *Issey Miyake Spectacle: Body Works*. Featuring the Japanese designer's avant-garde fashion creations, the show focused attention on the dynamic interplay between high fashion and fine art.

Picasso's *Guernica* on view in the Museum's rotunda in 1939

John R. Lane

On the acquisitions front, the most notable addition to the collection during Hopkins's tenure was Clyfford Still's gift of twenty-eight of his monumental paintings in 1975. As a result, SFMOMA became one of the first public institutions to own a substantial collection of work by this major Abstract Expressionist. The photography collection also grew dramatically during this period. Pioneering images by Man Ray, Ilse Bing, and Robert Frank augmented new work by Robert Adams, Larry Clark, Robert Mapplethorpe, and Joel-Peter Witkin.

John R. Lane, formerly director of the Carnegie Museum of Art in Pittsburgh, was named director in 1987. Bringing to SFMOMA a distinct vision of the heightened role it should play in the cultural life of the Bay Area and beyond, he led the Museum's efforts to embark on a new era of growth and consolidation.

Under Lane's direction, the Curatorial Division undertook an accelerated exhibition schedule. A focus on contemporary painting and sculpture led to shows of work by Sigmar Polke (1990), Luciano Fabro (1992), and Jeff Koons (1992). The Photography Department offered exhibitions by John Coplans (1988), Sebastião Salgado (1990), Helen Levitt (1991), Wright Morris (1992), and Dorothea Lange (1994). The Department of Architecture and Design originated major regional shows, including *Visionary San Francisco* (1990) and *The Color of Elements: The Architecture of Mark Mack* (1993). Among the notable media-based exhibitions were *Bay Area Media* (1990), *The Projected Image* (1991), and *Thresholds and Enclosures: Television as Sculpture* (1993).

The permanent collection flourished after the establishment of the Accessions Committee Fund in 1987, which provided the Museum with its first substantial acquisitions budget. However, the Museum still relies heavily on the generosity of its donors. One of the most important gifts in the Museum's history was the bequest of Elise Stern Haas in 1991. Comprising some thirty works by leading artists of the modern era, this bequest gave SFMOMA its most renowned painting, Matisse's *Femme au chapeau*. Other important gifts to the collection include the over twenty important artworks purchased for the Museum from 1997 to 1999 by Trustee Phyllis Wattis, the promised gift of the Djerassi Klee Collection, the establishment in 1998 of the Prentice and Paul Sack Photographic Trust of approximately one thousand nineteenth- and twentieth-century photographs, and the fractional and promised gift by Bay Area collectors Vicki and Kent Logan of more than three hundred contemporary artworks.

The growing number of acquisitions underscored the inadequacy of the Civic Center quarters, which could display no more than ten percent of the permanent collection. In the late 1980s, Lane and the Board of Trustees agreed that the Museum needed a new home—in a new building of international stature. In July 1988 SFMOMA announced plans to construct a facility in the Yerba Buena Gardens neighborhood, the eighty-seven-acre, mixed-use redevelopment project adjacent to the Moscone Convention Center south of Market Street.

David A. Ross

Two months later, the Trustees' Architect Selection Committee announced that Swiss architect Mario Botta had been chosen to design the new building. Two years later, in September 1990, Botta unveiled his design for a 225,000-square-foot modernist structure. The powerful new building would double the gallery space of the Museum's home in the War Memorial Veterans Building. Made possible by a successful $95 million capital campaign—the largest fund-raising effort by a California cultural institution to date—the new building was completed in the summer of 1994. The opening celebration took place on January 18, 1995, sixty years after SFMOMA first opened its doors on Van Ness Avenue. In 1997, after leading the institution through ten years of unprecedented growth, Lane left the Museum and was succeeded in June 1998 by David A. Ross. The sixth director of the Museum, Ross had previously served as director of the Whitney Museum of American Art in New York City.

The SFMOMA permanent collection embraces the entire span of twentieth-century art and in photography, extends back to the founding of the medium in the 1900s. Significant early modernist works, an internationally renowned collection of photography, important holdings of media- and time-based works, architecture and design objects, and a distinguished selection of work by contemporary regional, national, and international artists testify to its quality. Since its establishment in 1935, the Museum has been a leading force in promoting the development and appreciation of contemporary art in San Francisco.

SFMOMA looks forward to contributing to the artistic vitality of the Bay Area in the twenty-first century, for the vision of its first director, Grace McCann Morley, is still relevant. As she stated in a 1958 memo to the Board of Trustees, "A museum of contemporary art must lead the way, it must explore, it must endeavor to reach out into the new fields of art as they develop, it must try to assure a firm foundation of understanding for the new of yesterday that has become the accepted of today and will be the tradition of tomorrow."

Mario Botta sketches
SFMOMA in 1997.

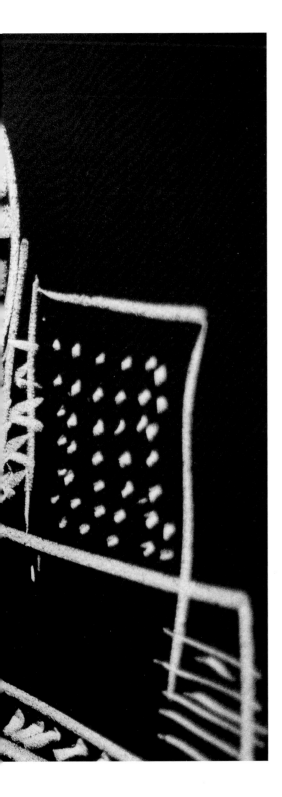

The Architect Selection Committee's choice of Mario Botta as the SFMOMA project architect came after extensive interviews with several prominent architects and visits to the offices and completed projects of the three finalists—Mario Botta, Frank Gehry, and Thomas Beeby. The site visits were a revelation to the committee. "Botta's work was so near to our expectations and wishes that it was evident he would be the best choice for this project," stated John Lane, who joined Board of Trustees Chairman Brooks Walker, Jr., in announcing the selection in 1988.

Botta's building for SFMOMA derives its power from many sources: the masterly orchestration of pure geometric form on a grand scale, the integration of plain materials such as brick and sheetrock with the richer textures of stone and marble, and the subtle workings of light in elegant, well-proportioned galleries. And yet Botta's design is simple, *modern* in the best sense of the word, referring to the judicious use of form to express function. At SFMOMA, "function" encompasses the need to provide an artistic showcase, an aesthetic sanctuary, and a community gathering place—the art museum reinvented as town square and temple. Botta's inspired combination of forms and textures accommodates activities ranging from art-viewing to shopping to partying, all enhanced by a light-drenched atrium of breathtaking size—a volume that infuses the interior with a sense of grandeur.

The consistency of Botta's design approach imparts to his completed projects a staying power—an elemental timelessness and gravitas—that is rare in the trend-driven world of contemporary architecture. Fortunately for San Francisco and its art community, this quality is fully evident in SFMOMA. Botta's stated aim for the Museum was that it should attain "that perfect balance where architecture and art enrich one another." With restraint and dignity, the building evokes the sublime, enduring values of great art and architecture, serving as a stable foundation for the restless changeability, the state of permanent flux, that characterizes the contemporary art world.

Botta derives his powers, in part, from a paradox: This avowed modernist is also a traditionalist, with roots in the rich earth of European classicism as well as in Modernism. He comes from the canton of Ticino in the southern Alps. Although Ticino lies on the Swiss side of the border, its cultural roots are Italian. The first great architect to hail from Ticino was Francesco Borromini (1599–1677), master of the Baroque.

Botta studied architecture in Venice with Carlo Scarpa, an admirer of the work of American architect Frank Lloyd Wright. (More than one critic has noted in SFMOMA echoes of Wright's Guggenheim Museum.) Prior to setting up his office in Lugano in 1969, Botta worked in the studios of two acknowledged modern masters: Le Corbusier and Louis I. Kahn. Kahn's Kimbell Museum in Fort Worth, Texas, has been described as one of the most exquisitely illuminated buildings of the twentieth century.

House, Stabio, Switzerland, 1980

Ransila 1 Building, Lugano, Switzerland, 1981–85

Botta began his career designing relatively modest hillside homes in
Ticino. Even then, his projects displayed a singular clarity, an elemental force
evoked by the use of brick and stone to make dense, minimal geometric
forms with symmetrical window openings, cutouts, and other unique formal
elements. During the 1980s Botta's powerful, distinctive structures earned
him an international reputation, leading to commissions such as the Mediathèque in Villeurbanne, France, and the Ransila 1 Building in Lugano. Botta's
inventive use of traditional, basic materials such as stone, brick, and concrete
masonry—as seen in the interior of the State Bank in Fribourg, Switzerland—
and his graceful massing of spare yet weighty geometric volumes became
recognized as the hallmarks of his architectural style. At a church in Mogno,
Switzerland, these elements attained a degree of harmony that elevated the
work to a more majestic level. Botta's design for this church—a perfect cylinder cut at a sharp angle—and his cylindrical church in the Paris suburb of Evry
are the predecessors of the striking black-and-white striped skylight at
SFMOMA.

Mediathèque, Villeurbanne, France, 1984–88

State Bank, Fribourg, Switzerland, 1977–82 (main hall)

Cathedral, Evry, France, 1988–95

San Giovanni Battista Church, Mogno, Switzerland, 1986–96

Top left:
Botta's first design for the
Museum included a ring of
trees around the skylight.

Top right and bottom:
Mario Botta's final model
for the Museum

Botta's first completed model of the building won great acclaim when he unveiled it in September 1990. This would remain the fundamental design, with few subsequent changes. The ring of trees Botta had envisioned to encircle the prominent oculus was excised, and the staircase angling up one side of the building—a required safety feature transformed into a striking design element—took on a slightly different form. But the essential structure was unmodified: an imposing, red brick building, its fortress-like mass leavened by setbacks and, more significantly, by the enormous truncated turret topped with a slanted window at the center.

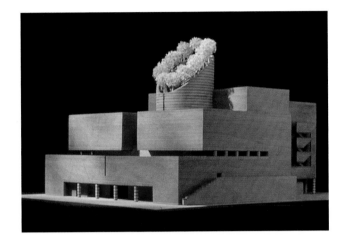

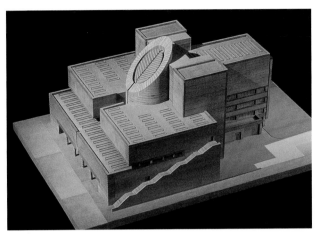

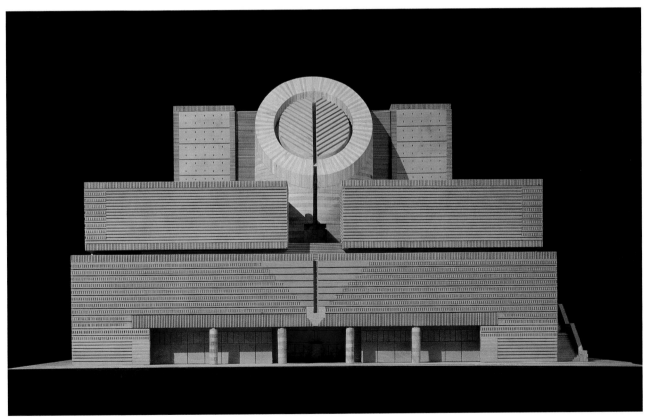

Botta's sketch shows his vision of the Museum building as a strong presence within the city's skyline.

The architect's early sketches and drawings reveal that he knew from the beginning what he wanted the building to look like, both inside and out, as well as in relation to its surroundings. The heart (and soul) of the Museum is the atrium, the grand central volume that soars 135 feet from the first floor to the skylit top of the central turret. Botta's balanced mix of natural and artificial light in the galleries takes its cue from the various types of artwork on display.

The Museum's striking shape, which makes the building such a powerful presence in the urban landscape, was in large measure generated by the

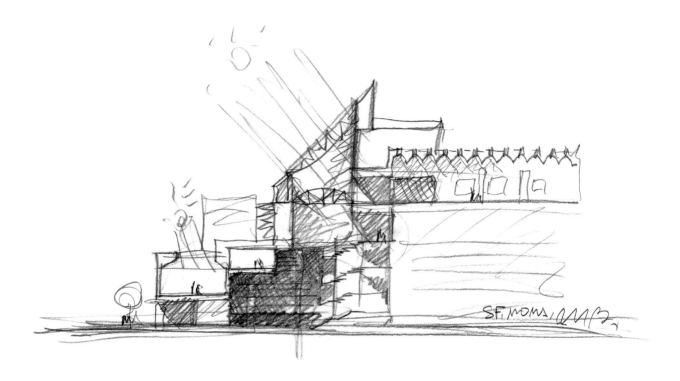

demands of site and program. As Botta explained, "The typology of a building is determined by two conditions: the function it must carry out and the site where it must rise." Along with considerations of site, Botta had considerable input from the entire staff, who developed a program delineating the functional problems in the old building and provided a wish list for the new one. Staff members measured gallery walls, calculated spatial requirements, and asked for generously proportioned volumes to accommodate the large scale of many modern and contemporary artworks.

In Botta's side elevation sketch each floor is stepped back from the preceding one to allow for natural light in the galleries and atrium.

The floor plans opposite indicate the distribution of space over five floors. Like a town square, the fifty-five hundred-square-foot central atrium is ringed by lively public spaces—store, café, theater, special-events room— and dominated by the grand staircase at rear center.

Accessed from elevators or the central staircase, the four floors of galleries above the ground floor provide fifty thousand square feet of display space. The thoughtfully orchestrated sequence of rooms has been designed to accommodate a diverse assortment of artworks. Only partially evident in the sequence of plans, these floors step back from the ground level in three tiers, providing access to natural light in the galleries and also serving to scale down the exterior mass of the building.

On view in the second-floor galleries are paintings and sculptures from the Museum's permanent collection, including areas devoted to California art and to architecture and design. Here a 210-foot-long enfilade, a sequence of skylit galleries, provides what is perhaps the most satisfying array of spaces in the entire building.

On the third floor, surrounding the central staircase and completely shielded from natural light, is a series of galleries where light-sensitive photographs and works on paper are displayed.

The fourth and fifth floors are devoted to special exhibitions and media-related installations. Here the spaces were designed to be as flexible as possible, permitting the display of large-scale works in all media. A bridge across the skylit turret provides dramatic, vertiginous access to the fifth-floor galleries; on the floor below, the architect carved out a small terrace that from time to time allows for the display of a large outdoor sculpture.

The basement level (not shown) provides space for art storage, a library, a graphic-arts study center, and a lecture hall, along with an area for art handling and receiving.

1

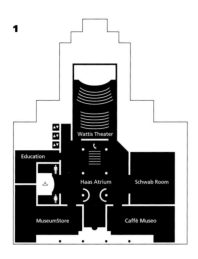

Wattis Theater

Education

Haas Atrium   Schwab Room

MuseumStore   Caffè Museo

2

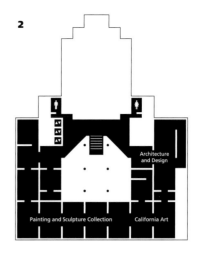

Architecture
and Design

Painting and Sculpture Collection   California Art

3

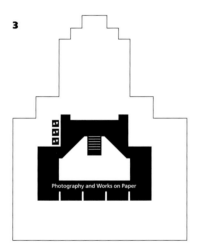

Photography and Works on Paper

4

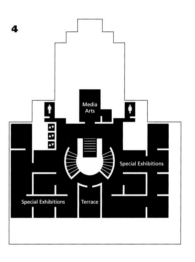

Media
Arts

Special Exhibitions

Special Exhibitions   Terrace

5

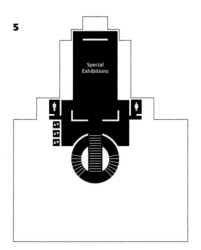

Special
Exhibitions

Several thousand people attended groundbreaking festivities, which included a performance by Survival Research Laboratories.

Following an intensive and highly successful fund-raising campaign and negotiations to secure the sixty thousand-square-foot site south of Market Street, the groundbreaking ceremony for the new Museum building took place in April 1992. The highest beam in the building's steel skeleton was put in place in January 1993. By June 1994, construction of the Museum was completed, except for the café and the special-events space. Three months later, the Museum permanently closed its Civic Center quarters. Finally, a team consisting of Botta; architect of record (and designer of the back-of-the-building spaces) Hellmuth, Obata & Kassabaum; project manager Bechtel International; and a construction team headed by general contractor Swinerton & Walberg managed the remarkable feat of completing the 225,000-square-foot project on time and on budget. The grand-opening celebration took place on January 18, 1995.

Rear view of Museum
during construction,
March 1993

Looking up toward the
fifth-floor bridge and
top of skylight during
construction, January
1993

View of Museum construc-
tion from the southwest,
February 1993

Opposite:
Glazing the skylight,
September 1993

The Museum as seen from Yerba Buena Gardens. Directly behind the Museum is Timothy Pfleuger's 1925 Pacific Telephone and Telegraph building. In the foreground are the Yerba Buena Center for the Arts buildings: the galleries (left), designed by Fumihiko Maki, and the theater (right), designed by James Stewart Polshek.

Those new to San Francisco and especially to SoMa, the neighbor-hood south of Market Street, will discover a lively, mixed-use district offering an array of cultural and entertainment venues. Facing the Museum are the Yerba Buena Gardens, home to the Yerba Buena Center for the Arts, designed by Fumihiko Maki, and the Center for the Arts Theater, designed by James Stewart Polshek. Romaldo Giurgola's five-acre garden, positioned atop the Moscone Convention Center, offers a verdant urban sanctuary, which features the Martin Luther King, Jr., Memorial by artist Houston Conwill. Just beyond the garden rises the Metreon, a complex containing theaters, restaurants, stores, and other diversions. Myriad hotels, restaurants, and nightclubs have also opened in recent years. The district, which does double duty as San Francisco's high-tech, dot-com start-up zone and as a burgeoning cultural center, represents urban living at its best.

Those who know the city well have perhaps an even greater appreciation of the transformation south of Market, for in the not-so-distant past this district was known as Skid Row, with dingy SRO hotels, flophouses, bars, and other down-at-the-heels establishments lining the streets. For several decades, successive city governments and shifting concepts of urban planning kept the neighborhood in limbo. Bits and pieces did manage to fall into place, notably the Moscone Convention Center, which opened in 1981, and, by the end of the eighties, a few new hotels. However, no real overall vision for the district had emerged—none, at least, that people were willing to support.

The Museum helped change all that. Today Skid Row has been transformed into a culture "gulch" as well as a high-tech haven, and this radical improvement can be attributed in no small measure to the presence of SFMOMA. When the Board of Trustees and Director John Lane made a commitment to the site in 1991, it sent the clearest possible signal that SoMa was on its way.

Botta's design offers an appropriately measured response to the mixed-use, mixed-scale style of the SoMa neighborhood. The structure's imposing mass and volume and its pure architectonic presence enable SFMOMA to hold its own near a sea of downtown skyscrapers. At the same time, the subtle yet lively decorative patterning of the exterior brickwork, the setbacks, and especially the bold, black-and-white striped, glass-topped cylinder rising from the center lend it an inviting, street-friendly appearance in keeping with the low-rise structures in and around the Yerba Buena Gardens across the street. SoMa is an area with numerous older buildings as well as newer hotels, high-rises, and sleek, archi-techno creations like the Metreon. SFMOMA, for all its Modernism and architectural monumentality, demonstrates in its burnt-sienna-colored brick exterior Botta's fealty to traditional ways of making a building. In doing so, it creates a link between the Museum and the older, utilitarian structures in the neighborhood.

The brick exterior (a veneer of pre-cast brick panels attached to structural concrete for reasons of seismic safety) exerts a subtle visual appeal. Parallel courses of brick extend horizontally across the lower part of the facade forming the shape of an arrowhead and drawing attention to the Museum's main entrance. These patterned bands of bricks wrap around the facade; on the second tier, similar brickwork defines and decorates the corners, while narrow reveals reemphasize the building's horizontality. A simpler pattern of corner reveals and a grid of indentations adorn the uppermost tier, providing a quiet counterpoint to the bold stripes and the glowing, angled skylight. On the south wall (now blocked from view by a neighboring building), a dramatic staircase cascades gracefully down the side of the structure —a required safety feature transformed into another inspired design element. These subtle, almost delicate embellishments temper as well as play off the building's monumentality.

Multiple elements serve to focus attention on the building's front entrance. The paired glass doors, on a direct axis with the entrance to the Yerba Buena Gardens across the street, are aligned with the vertical glass slot above, which bisects the structure. Patterns in the brick take the form of an arrowhead, directing attention to the doors, which are quite small in scale relative to the mass of the building. For the convenience of visitors, a generous patio has been carved out of the ground floor, extending the public space of the sidewalk and providing shelter for those waiting to enter the Museum. The patio also offers *al fresco* seating at Caffè Museo, flanking the entrance.

The main entrance may appear rather undramatic for such a large, powerful building. However, once visitors pass through the glass doors, the reason for this understated quality becomes evident. The doors open directly into the soaring, light-filled atrium. The transition from the low-ceilinged entrance to the atrium's grand volume is breathtaking.

Looking down into the
atrium from the third-floor
galleries

Previous pages:
Two views of the central
staircase from the atrium

Soaring to a height of 135 feet from the main floor to the top of the slanted glass crown of the skylight, SFMOMA's atrium is among the finest museum spaces built in the twentieth century. Mario Botta accurately describes it as "the true heart of the building . . . the center of spatial gravity for the entire museum." With the grand staircase at the rear rising ziggurat-like into the turret, the luminous volume has the spiritual quality of a temple interior. And yet the atrium remains a lively space, a gathering place for people-watching and interaction. Surrounded by the busy activity zones that characterize the modern museum—café, store, theater, classroom, checkroom, special-event rooms—the atrium serves as the building's town square, although it might more appropriately be called a piazza, given Botta's penchant for Italianate textures and finishes.

The abundance of striping particularly evokes a piazza, lending graphic liveliness to the rich materials. The flooring and column bases consist of alternating bands of polished black and dark gray Canadian granite; the same striated stone graces the staircase, drawing the eye upward. The dark tones of the atrium floor provide a striking contrast to the pale golden Nordic icebirch wainscoting and the white purity of the walls above.

Visitors chart their own paths through a museum, and there are many ways to experience SFMOMA. However, a stroll up or down the grand staircase should not be missed, for this is the most dramatic route through the building. In contrast to the brightness of the atrium and turret, the staircases have subdued lighting from recessed overhead fixtures. At each level, spacious landings overlook the atrium, inviting people to linger. Rows of round ventilation holes and large circular cutouts braced with crosses embellish the white interior walls of the cylindrical turret. From the stairs and landings, and at other places throughout the building, narrow apertures offer glimpses of the city and the sky, while the fourth-floor terrace grants an expansive view over Yerba Buena Gardens. Between the fourth and fifth floors the stairs wrap around the turret, providing access to one of the Museum's most distinctive elements—the fifth-floor bridge. The trip across the thirty-eight-foot-long, white-painted bowstring truss bridge has been known to cause vertigo; otherwise the experience is sheer delight. Visitors find themselves bathed in golden white light, encircled by glowing white walls, poised beneath the diaphanous leaf pattern traced into the skylight's slanting glass roof, with a view of the sky above and the atrium seventy-five feet below.

Opposite and following pages: Views of the turret and fifth-floor bridge

The purpose of the building's introverted orientation becomes evident when touring the four floors of galleries, which more or less surround the turret. This is a building designed not to show itself off or to frame outward views, but rather to display art—which it does with flair and finesse. For Botta, viewing art in a museum is a kind of religious experience. That belief is clearly evident in SFMOMA's fifty thousand square feet of galleries, all of which are suffused with a lucid, almost spiritual calm and clarity.

Many visitors find that the best place to begin their tour through the galleries is on the fifth floor, accessed from either the turret bridge or the elevators. Intended for the mounting of special exhibitions, the fifth-floor galleries were designed as a single volume, 55 feet by 112 feet; however, the space is often subdivided to meet the requirements of the particular works being shown. The 23½-foot-high ceilings have coffers with built-in light fixtures and specially designed skylights that together provide a controlled, perfectly modulated mix of natural and artificial light. These fixtures have been installed in all the skylit galleries throughout the Museum. Mario Botta explained his design for the lighting of these galleries: "Natural light is a specific element tied to a geographic location. . . . The artworks on display will be viewed through the 'real light' of the city. With filters and veils, you can control and modulate light through skylights, thereby offering optimum conditions while also leaving the walls completely available as expository surfaces."

Overleaf:
The fifth-floor galleries

The Museum is designed to
accommodate a variety of
art, as can be seen in these
installation views (from left)
of work by contemporary
Dutch designers, and by
artists Bill Viola and
Alexander Calder.

The Museum's top two
floors are ideally suited to
the display of large-scale
works by artists as diverse
as (from left) Jim Hodges,
Richard Diebenkorn, and
Wenda Gu.

On the fourth floor, the ceilings reach a height of eighteen feet, making them ideally suited for the display of large-scale contemporary art. Also on this floor are the media arts galleries. Equipped with a support-hanging grid, independent lighting, a control room, and a high concentration of electrical and audio outlets, these galleries offer a completely flexible environment for installations, including film, video, and electronic and time-based media. The sculpture terrace tucked in front of the turret can be reached from this floor as well.

Presentations in the fourth-floor galleries of works by Stan Douglas and Thomas Struth (left) and by Ren Jian and Song Dong (above)

On the third floor, a series of small galleries uses only artificial light, as the works on paper and photographs on display here could be damaged by the ultraviolet component of natural light. To accommodate the usually small scale of such works, the architect scaled down the height of the ceiling to twelve feet.

Overleaf:
The 1999 presentation of
Full Moon: Apollo Mission Photographs of the Lunar Landscape in the third-floor galleries

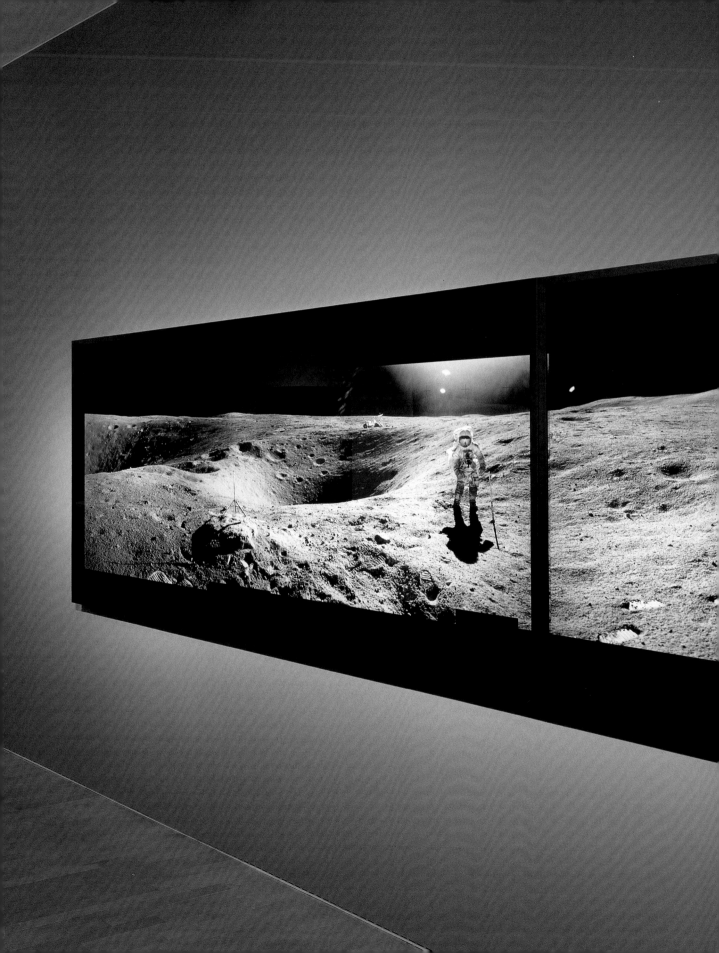

Works by Mark Rothko and Louise Bourgeois on view in the second-floor galleries.

Overleaf:
The intimate size of the first three second-floor galleries accommodates smaller-scale early–twentieth-century works by artists such as Pablo Picasso, Constantin Brancusi, Henri Matisse, and Max Pechstein.

On the second floor, the Museum's permanent collection of painting and sculpture is exhibited in a series of galleries arranged in a 210-foot-long enfilade paralleling the front of the building. This classical, conservative arrangement of exhibition spaces recalls the layout of several of the great royal museums in Europe, such as the Louvre and the Hermitage. As the impressive setting for SFMOMA's collection of twentieth-century works by such artists as Clyfford Still, Mark Rothko, Jackson Pollock, and Robert Motherwell, these galleries help to affirm their stature as modern masters. Also located on this level is the architecture and design collection, which is housed in less dramatic but generously scaled galleries just beyond the rooms devoted to California artists. Located between the painting and sculpture and the architecture and design galleries is an interactive study room equipped with state-of-the-art computers programmed for hands-on multimedia exploration of collections and exhibitions.

Preceding pages:
The Museum's painting
and sculpture collection
includes works by Josef
Albers, Georgia O'Keeffe,
Joseph Stella, Mark Rothko,
Louise Bourgeois, Diego
Rivera, Sargent Johnson,
and Stuart Davis.

Afternoon light pours
through a narrow window
flanked by two Jasper
Johns works (above), while
it gently filters through the
skylights atop the enfilade
of galleries (at left, looking toward a Richard
Diebenkorn painting).

True to Botta's intention, the Evelyn and Walter Haas, Jr., Atrium serves as a multipurpose space. Not only the crossroads and primary focal point for museum-goers, the atrium has become one of the most popular locations in San Francisco for large-scale private parties, benefits, and all manner of social events. It also functions as a spectacular exhibition space, especially for art that can take full advantage of the soaring space.

When a retrospective of Alexander Calder's work was presented in 1998, one of his mobiles was suspended from the bridge and reached almost all the way down to the atrium floor. The following year, a striking sculpture by Cai Guo-qiang hung in the atrium as part of the exhibition *Inside Out: New Chinese Art*. In early 2000, the Museum commissioned a new pair of wall drawings by Conceptual artist Sol LeWitt as part of a major career retrospective.

Works by Alexander Calder, Sol LeWitt, and Cai Guo-qiang in the atrium

Botta's design for the MuseumStore enhances the town-square ambience of the atrium. Reflecting the great success of the store since its opening, the original 3,200-square-foot space will be expanded to 5,500 square feet. Along with museum-goers who stop by the store before or after visiting the galleries are other patrons for whom the store itself is the main attraction. Finished in Nordic icebirch and illuminated with custom-designed lighting fixtures, the store utilizes the windows facing the street for eye-catching displays of merchandise.

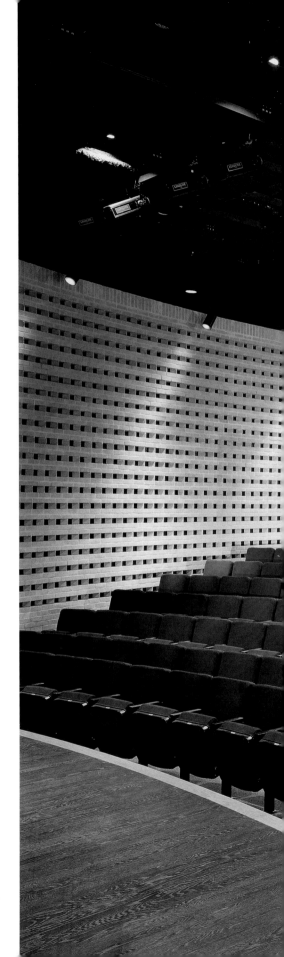

Adjoining the atrium via a pair of sliding Nordic icebirch panels, the
Schwab Room can be configured for both intimate and large-scale activities.
Elegant design details—including the slatted maple ceiling, custom barrel
vaults, and lighting fixtures designed by Botta—make it the ideal setting for
both public and private art openings, parties, receptions, and meetings.

Lectures, symposia, musical performances, and other events take place
in the Phyllis Wattis Theater, a 278-seat, 6,200-square-foot space located
behind the grand staircase on the atrium level. The theater has projection
equipment for film, video, and slide presentations. Concrete masonry walls
enclose the space, with every third course set at an angle to facilitate the
absorption of sound by means of a concealed acoustic backing. Here Botta
has created a simple, handsome, and functional performance space.

The sleek interior and sidewalk terrace of Caffè Museo are a magnet for passersby on the street as well as for the many museum-goers taking a lunch or coffee break. For this 2,500-square-foot space, Botta has used the same alluring wood, glass, and stone finishes that adorn the other atrium-level spaces. Light fixtures are built into the slotted maple ceiling, and the tables and chairs were custom-designed by the architect.

Botta's design for the Museum includes space for offices, a conservation studio, meeting rooms, and other "behind the scenes" facilities. These semi-public and private work spaces also have a mix of artificial and natural light, reinforcing the humanistic architectural philosophy that inspired SFMOMA's design. The diverse nongallery spaces break down as follows: classrooms and studios, 3,000 square feet; library, 3,800 square feet; conservation studio, 3,000 square feet; art study, handling, and storage, 15,000 square feet; offices, 22,500 square feet; and private parking, 15,000 square feet. Located on the lower level, the library contains more than 85,000 books, catalogues, and periodicals, and is open to the public by appointment. The lower level also houses the art storage, receiving, and handling areas, along with facilities for maintaining the building's state-of-the-art temperature and humidity control systems, which are crucial to the preservation of artworks.

Owing to the large scale of many contemporary works, one of the most important functional elements in the modern museum is an oversize freight elevator. The one at SFMOMA—twenty feet wide, twelve feet deep, and twelve feet high—does the job handily.

Works in paintings storage, such as these by Yves Klein, Anne Appleby, and Harry Rosenthal (above) are hung on sliding galvanized-steel panels.

Overleaf:
The Museum's freight elevator with Dara Birnbaum's *Tiananmen Square: Break-in Transmission* (1988–90) in the foreground

Preceding pages:
A photograph from the
exhibition *Full Moon:
Apollo Mission Photo-
graphs of the Lunar Land-
scape* under ultraviolet light
in the Elise S. Haas Conservation Studio. Ultraviolet
examination is used as a
nonintrusive way to distin-
guish between different
materials in a work
of art.

H97" L59" W46"

↑
UP

↑
UP

↑
UP

INN
3.3

A·R·T·E·X

DEGAS TO PICASSO

Brooklyn
MoA
CAT # 92

12/20

BACK

FRAGILE

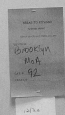

www.sfmoma.org

Library of Congress Catalogue Card Number: 00–131478
ISBN: 0-918471-59-1

Editor: Janet Wilson
Designer: Ed Marquand
Assistant Designer: Vivian Larkins
Production: Marquand Books, Inc., Seattle

Front cover:
Detail of the SFMOMA exterior
Back cover:
Detail of the grand staircase

Frontispieces:
Page 1: View of the turret from the fifth-floor bridge
Pages 2–3: View of the Museum's turret and skylight
illuminated from within
Pages 4–5: The skylight and bridge seen from below
Pages 6–7: The Museum's fourth-floor galleries wrap
around the central turret.
Page 8: Close-up view of the Museum's turret with the
1925 Pacific Telephone and Telegraph building in the
background

Photo credits:
Unless listed here, all photographs are by Richard Barnes,
© San Francisco Museum of Modern Art, Richard Barnes.
Page 12: Dan Escobar; pp. 14, 16, 17: courtesy SFMOMA
archives; p. 18: Timothy Greenfield-Sanders; p. 19:
Lena Bertucci; pp. 20–21: Pino Musi; p. 22: (left) Roberto
Sellitto; (right) Archivo Mario Botta; p. 23: (top left, bottom
left and right) Pino Musi; p. 23: (top right) Alo Zanetta;
p. 25: Peter Xiques; pp. 26–27: copy photo by Ben
Blackwell; p. 30: Marvin Collins; p. 31: (left) Jo Fielder;
(center) Michael Jang; pp. 32–33: Perretti & Park; pp. 62–
65, 67, 80: Ian Reeves.

Printed and bound in Singapore by CS Graphics Pte., Ltd.